# The Verve

# The Verve

## PHOTOGRAPHS BY CHRIS FLOYD

REEL ART PRESS

# FOREWORD

When every modern move creates a glut of data, looking back on photographs shot on film at the end of the 20th century feels closer to studying cave painting than to anything happening today. As we drift on a sea of souvenirs and images of every moment, confusion reigns. The prehistoric artists, by a certain measure, enjoyed a clearer picture.

What a thing it is, then, to behold an un-faded but still ageing photograph and say that you were there. To remember, more or less, what went on.

Between 1994 and 1998 myself and Chris Floyd toured with, hung around and otherwise inflicted ourselves on the four (and sometimes five) members of The Verve (or Verve as we first knew them) as they ascended from cool to colossal before falling apart in the time honoured fashion.

We had no foresight of this trajectory. But Chris had a camera. The excitement and enthusiasm that drove us (to say nothing of the publishing industry that paid us) are hard to capture now, but the images abide. Those years, it turns out, were the twilight of analogue consciousness and certain seeming certainties about the world at large. Whatever we are now, we were not then. This isn't just the everyday past we're looking at, but another planet.

The official histories of the era, sombre documents mostly, seem inclined to sweep all the exuberance of those days into shame and shade. As though a few more early nights might have changed the course of economic history or the flight paths of certain planes.

Those frowning cultural memoirs (and the testimony of some of the protagonists) submit the life of this band to the same sombre assessment as the decade. I must confess that the years of distance have yet to offer me any such certainty beyond a single subjective but abiding sense that blooms again when I look at these pictures: my god it was fun.

Sifting in hindsight through a period lived without foresight, I'm afraid a salute to the exuberance is the best I can do. As the song suggests, it is tonight we seek to be rock and roll stars, not years hence. To rock out with an eye for retrospect seems flawed at concept level. Perhaps this is what makes it all so photogenic. And not a camera phone in sight.

That said, we must admit to this: few on those tour buses or in those dressing rooms could say they were untouched by images of a golden age which had already gone. When you first get the call saying you're going to tour America, all the dream baggage of the 1950s, 60s and 70s flashes bright before you.

Those ideas, images and sounds are what get us into this mess, learning guitar, developing film, writing . . . with a view to it taking you somewhere. When you hit the road it's a dream come true. What happens on it is another matter. So I find myself looking back nostalgically to something that was, even as it happened, fuelled by fantasy. As to reality, I have no idea where that's gone.

What you can see here is the group's journey from thrilled outsiders to bona fide phenomenon. The earliest of these pictures date from July 1994. The band was playing the second stage at Lollapalooza, a space literally outside the main arena, often in the car park. A set of scaffolding and monitors set up each day and broken down as the tour moved on. Chris and I went to four shows on that tour . . . Las Vegas, Denver, Kansas City and Minneapolis. The band played mid afternoon, often in high temperatures. The sound from the main stage overwhelmed what was happening outside. They were good shows, great sometimes. But there were decent reasons to be elsewhere and there were never more than a hundred people in the crowd.

Four summers later and the band are playing to 33,000 of their own fans in the grounds of Haigh Hall, Wigan. Their hometown. That's some ascension. Naturally it has its costs. This is what you can't really know as an observer, the deeper business. You see the results, but you don't see it coming. At least I didn't. I think that's why I like these pictures so much, there's a through line that suits my own remembrance. You catch glimpses here of private charisma, signs of an abiding warmth. Things less visible sometimes in a performer's public stance and too easily forgotten in the seriousness that followed.

I suspect Chris' instincts have always leant more toward portrait and landscape than bodies in motion. There's a pull here to the non-performance aspects of show business, the more quotidian, less contrived. Yet this is always an issue with photography, even when its practitioners seek to lift a veil they cast another kind of spell. Every myth busted is another mirage.

This is what I think about when I see the picture of Richard in amongst the *Wizard of Oz* tableau at the MGM Grand in Las Vegas. In the end you have to click your heels together, go home and grow up. But not right now perhaps, and certainly not then. We were miles away and glad of it. Likewise we look back and wonder if some part of us remained.

Like photography, the music business has been transformed by technology since these images were made. I don't hang out with young bands anymore but I am occasionally exposed to their wisdom, and things seem a lot more strategised now. Even the shamans have a spreadsheet, it seems. Do people get to loiter in the desert still? One would hope so. Maybe popular culture is forever in this balance, an awkward, ever revising contract between monetised immaturity and the pressure to move on.

No doubt everyone in these pictures would tell you a different story. Which is not to say that anyone would be wrong. In time the wise emerge and appear righteous. As for the foolish, there is nothing we can do but carry on. If you're lucky you realise your reality runs alongside many others. Truths, so much sought and maligned of late, must coexist with one another. Like different photographs. That was some trip we were on. I'm not even sure it's over.

**MICHAEL HOLDEN**

# INSIDE THE BUBBLE AND HALF A LIFETIME AGO

There's that line that Martin Sheen says in *Apocalypse Now*. "Never get out of the boat. Absolutely goddamn right."

Late 1996, maybe two or three weeks before Christmas. 117 Church Road, Barnes, London, SW13. Olympic Studios, oh wow, this is where The Rolling Stones recorded 'Sympathy For The Devil'. This room. This is history. Sitting on a leather sofa. Some pot plants here and there, bits of coloured fabric strung over the ceiling to soften the interrogatory harshness of the downlights. A large whiteboard with a grid drawn on it. On the left, a list of song titles, then a row of symbols, illustrations and drawings stretching across from each title. Each one representing an element of the constituent parts of the recording of that song. There is also a dog in the room, a black Labrador. A cup of tea in hand. You, not the dog.

Six minutes later and you've just heard 'Bittersweet Symphony' for the first time. No warning. You just came for a visit to say hello. Right out of the blue. Right out of the huge speakers that Olympic is famous for. Life defining. You wish you could go back and hear it again for the first time. What a thing with which to be involved. Astonishing. Your tea has gone cold.

A night in Sheffield. The first gig in two years. Emotion, power, sound, energy and groove. It's a communion. No one wants it to end. The next morning onwards to Glasgow. Barrowlands. They can make the floor move there if they like you enough. The Britannia Hotel, Manchester, finishing off the artwork. And a curry in Wolverhampton. Curry in Wolverhampton? Always reminds you of Aretha in *The Blues Brothers*. "Best damned chicken in the state."

The second stage at the Sam Boyd Silver Bowl, Las Vegas, July 1994. About 105 degrees of heat. Just plugging in when a lone voice from the sparse crowd milling around the stage calls out to nobody in particular, *"Man, I can't believe those guys are wearing cords."*

On tour, USA, 1997. An amorphous, compressed catalogue of sights, voices, sounds, faces. And also accents. Wherever you go, accents.

Twenty two hours of show day is tedium, *routine*. So much time just hanging around, *waiting*. This is the reality of touring but in time this is also what you fetishise. The romance of being free enough to be bored. *The day of the show is the show*. Wake up. Walk around, so much waiting around, phone a friend, get some food, maybe if you're with me we'll do some shopping. Nod off. Your camera bag is a pillow. Wake up and check that your shot rolls of film haven't fallen out of your pocket. Always, constantly, checking that you've got the film you shot. And keep normally exposed rolls separate from rolls that need to be pushed in the processing. Go outside and watch the crowd as they arrive and the venue fills up. People look at the pass round your neck, your ACCESS ALL AREAS pass that is like Willy Wonka's golden ticket to the people who wonder what you are there for. Why have *you* got *that*?

The colours of dressing room walls permanently colour code specific cities in the memory. Washington D.C. and Seattle are green, Chicago is red, New York is beige, Sheffield is orange, Detroit has no colour but a beautiful oak floor, and San Francisco will always be a place papered with vintage promotional posters from 1970s adult movies.

On the bus. *Lord of the Flies* crossed with *Das Boot*. A silver aluminium submarine with a western landscape painting on the side of it. Husband and wife driver tag team. Non stop, Atlanta to Los Angeles, via Washington D.C., New York City, Boston, Detroit, Toronto, Chicago, Seattle and San Francisco. Snatches of sound from video tapes playing on the onboard VCR. The tracking is busted. Jean Luc Godard's *One Plus One*. That flat, neutral voiceover in between footage of The Rolling Stones recording 'Sympathy For The Devil' at Olympic Studios.

Lying in your bunk on the bus at 3 a.m. as you glide horizontally through the California night at 65mph, 'Dirt' by The Stooges playing in the blue lit womb of the front lounge, leading you on to Los Angeles, the end of the line and a

reckoning. That's the sound of travelling across the heartland by chrome bullet.

Truck stops in the middle of the night. Souvenir carousels selling plastic fish mounted on plinths that sing 'Macarena'. Trucker's Comfort jeans with 48-inch waists in a shade of blue that doesn't exist off the highway. Eggs and hash browns on oval plates, barely toasted toast. Jelly or jam? A 12 ounce strip steak in Chicago for breakfast, joyless and generic black coffee, coffee that never runs out, endless free refills and massive sugar shakers. All the time a man on a table nearby, absolute dead ringer for Allen Ginsberg. A handwritten check with numbers like hieroglyphics that always seem to add up to about 48 dollars. Divide that by nine and get back on the bus. Six hundred and seventy-three miles to go.

Chicago, you're so cold you buy another coat to wear over your normal coat. A charcoal grey peacoat with a black collar. You keep it for years until it won't do the mileage anymore.

Indoor smoking, all the time. Finding a laundry within a block's walk of the hotel on a day off and the excitement of getting everything washed and returned the same day, free of the stale smoke crust.

No mobile phones, no email, so nobody back home knows a thing of your whereabouts or situation. You buy postcards to collect and keep rather than send. *Ohio - The Buckeye State!*

Backstage at The Warfield, San Francisco. The man who designed so many of the great posters of the psychedelic era comes in to meet the band. They discuss the idea of him designing one for The Verve.

Richard points at you and says, "If you need any pictures of us to work from then get them from him. He's on the road with us, taking our souls away every night with his camera."

"Yeah," adds Simon Jones, "but we get them back on contact sheets."

**CHRIS FLOYD**

Verve will be
signing autographs
at our booth
after their set
(aprox. 30 MIN. after)
COME SEE 👁👁

VERVE

2A 3

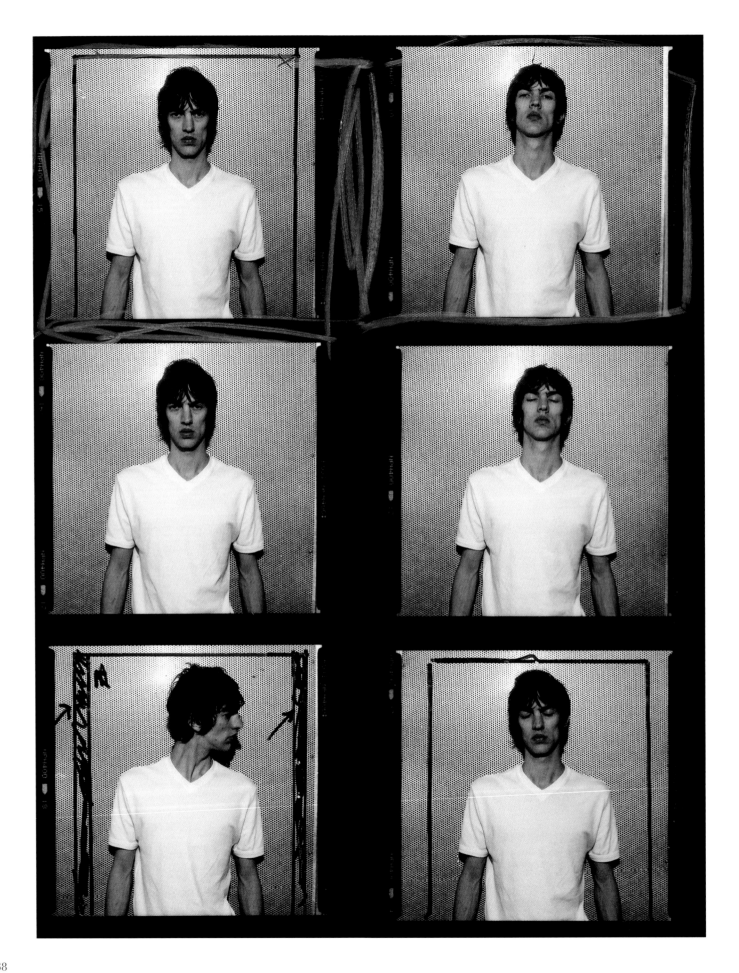

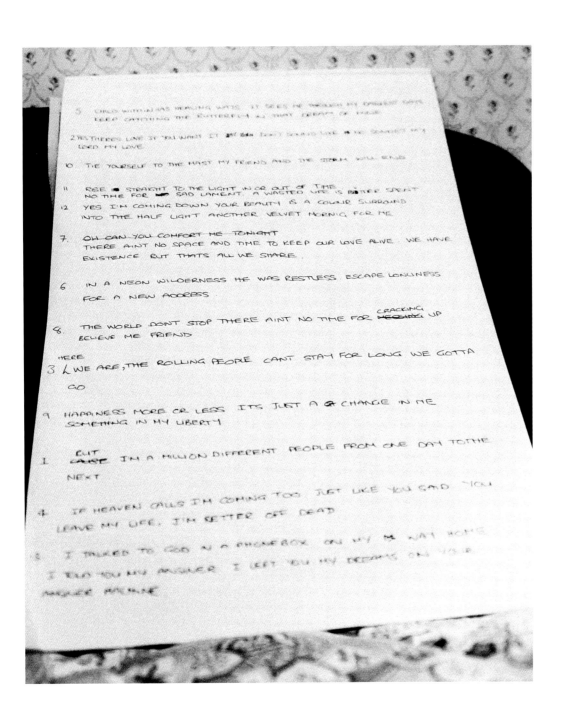

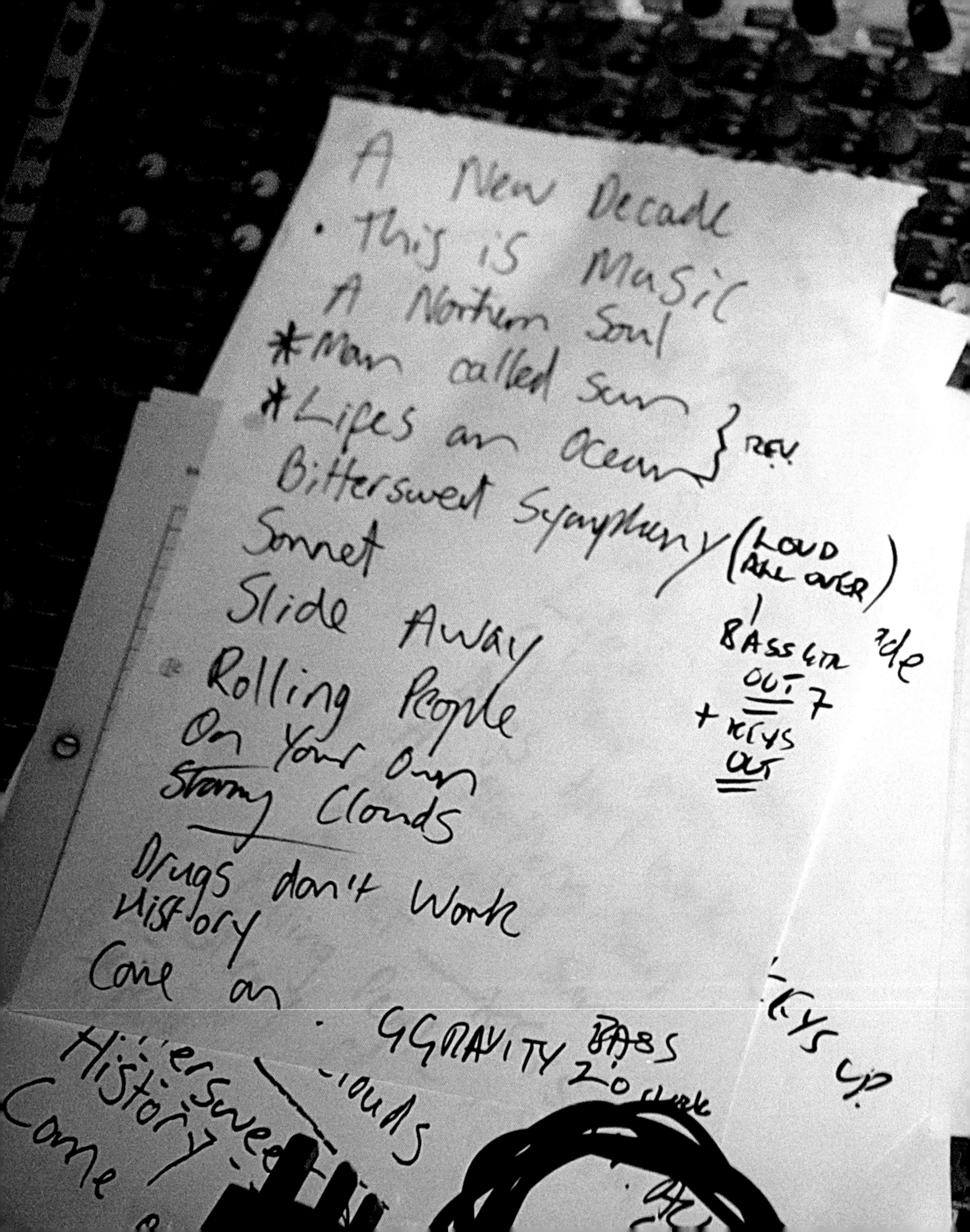

A New Decade
• This is Music
A Northern Soul
❋ Man called Sun ⎫
❋ Lifes an Ocean ⎬ REV
Bittersweet Symphony (LOUD
                        (ALL OVER) )
Sonnet                        ide
Slide Away              BASS GTR
○ Rolling People         OUT 7
On Your Own             + KEYS
Stormy Clouds            OUT

Drugs don't Work
History
Come on
                    • GGRAVITY BASS        KEYS UP
Bittersweet            2.0 clock
History              ...ouds
Come

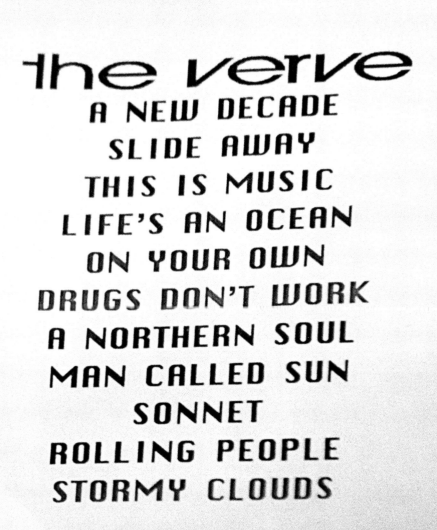

# the verve

A NEW DECADE
SLIDE AWAY
THIS IS MUSIC
LIFE'S AN OCEAN
ON YOUR OWN
DRUGS DON'T WORK
A NORTHERN SOUL
MAN CALLED SUN
SONNET
ROLLING PEOPLE
STORMY CLOUDS

---

BITTERSWEET
HISTORY
COME ON /G/G

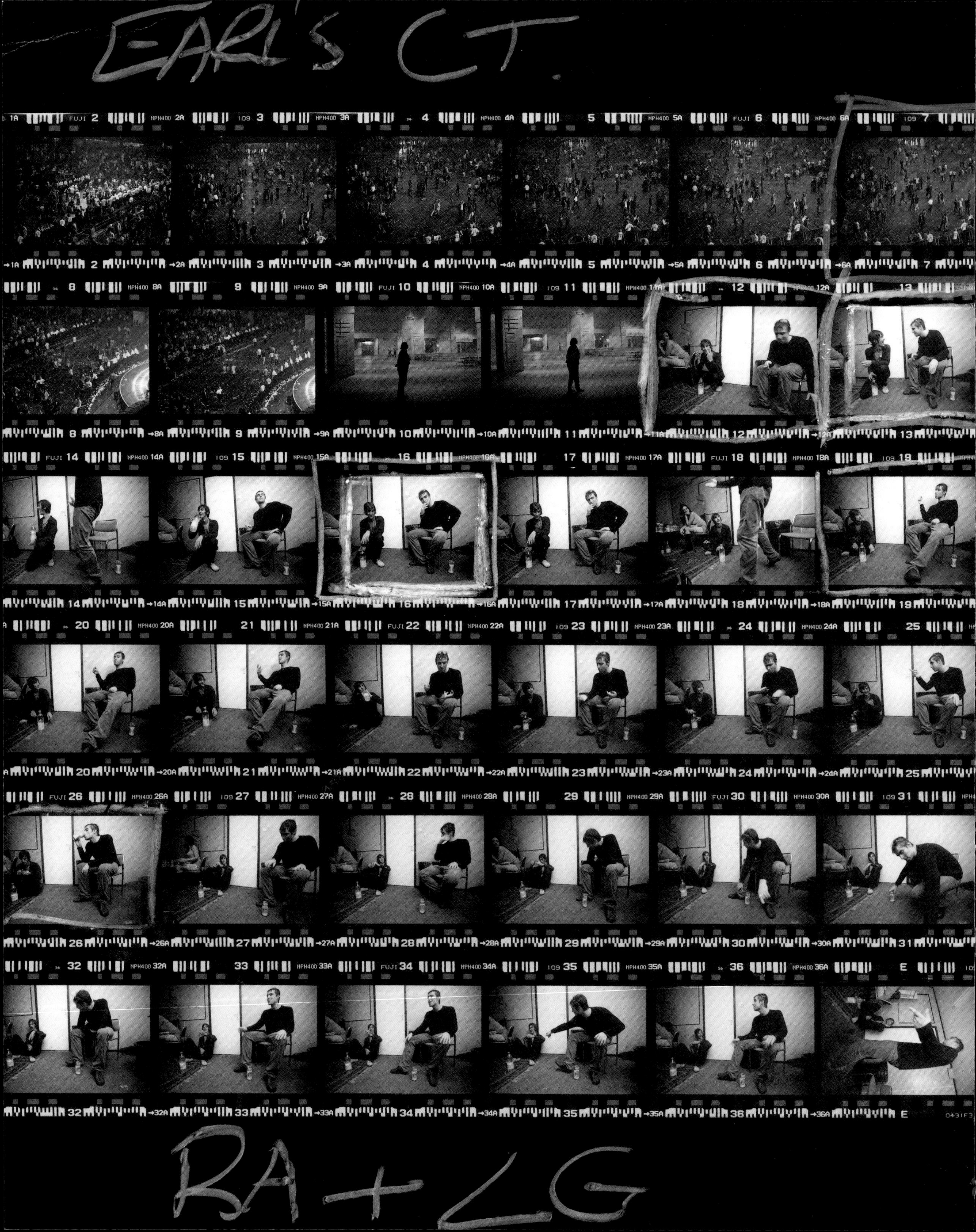
EARL'S CT.
RA + LG

Dear Chris Floyd

## <u>Re: Earl's Court - Photographing The Verve</u>

This is to confirm that you will receive an Access All Areas pass to photograph The Verve on stage, backstage and in their dressing room at Earl's Court on 25/26/27 October 1997.

By signing below, you confirm that you will not take any photos of Oasis. Nor must you be in or take any photos of anyone in the production office and other work areas.

You are permitted to take photos of The Verve if they are talking to Oasis, however Ignition will have to give approval should any of these images want to be used by The Verve, Management and/or the Record Company.

Please do not enter the venue until after 17.30pm each night.

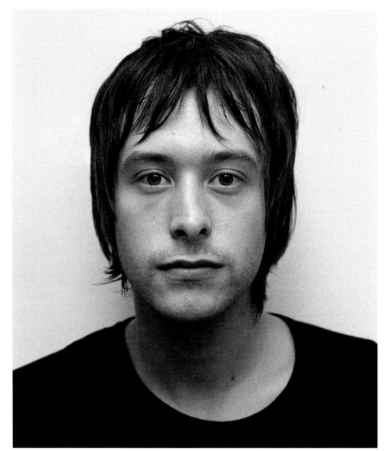

95

TODAY WAS MORE OR LESS THE same as yesterday. Boring basically! Emma and I have made a friend, John. The only lad and the only one I got on with! Emma sort of did but they chased each other around with pens trying to draw on each other.

It really started when Emma was playing on his Tamagotchi cyber pet, George. I was writing MUFC Rule all over the white board and he came over and wrote LFC (Urgh!!!) all over it! We just got talking and he told me his dog was called Tess and he lives in St Helens and his dad's called John too and he's got a little brother.

When everybody went home, Miss T dropped me and Emma off outside McDonald's in Wigan for tea coz we were staying there until the concert. We got lost and went and got me a CD, 'Bitter Sweet Symphony'.

I like John. Not fancy him. He's just sort of nice. If he was my age he could be a possibility but he's not. I want his phone number but there are so many people called J. Harris in St Helens. I'll probably never see him again now. **TESS SIMPSON**

IT WAS ABOUT 1994, WHEN I WAS 17, that one of my friends first introduced me to The Verve. He said they were the best band in the world. Given I was into Nirvana and Pearl Jam I thought, "I don't think the best band in the world is four blokes from Wigan who you saw in Bradford". He convinced me to go and see them at the Duchess pub in Leeds in 1995. Tickets were a fiver.

I don't think *Urban Hymns* had been released when we got tickets for their return gig at the Leadmill in 1997. It was an astonishing performance. Richard had gone from a fairly static frontman the last time I saw them to completely owning the stage. His confidence in the band, the music, the songs and himself was amazing to witness. No one had heard the songs before that night, I don't think, but it was obvious at first listen that it was a work of genius.

After the gig, dripping with sweat, no-one could stop smiling. My friend said, "I think it's the best stuff they've ever done. What do you think?" I replied, "I think it's the best gig I've ever been to." And I meant it. **ANDREW COX**

I WAS VISITING MY AUNT AND UNCLE in London, NW3, from Manchester. Oasis had always been my band, and part of that was our shared football team. Noel happened to live in those days in his famous Supernova Heights gaff, which was on Steele's Road – a 10 minute walk from my aunt and uncle's house. I'd heard that sometimes he'd chat to fans who waited for him, so I thought I would go up there. It was 4 September 1997 – I remember because City had won 3-1 at Forest the night before and I thought, ha, I'll have something to talk to him about!

I had my City shirt on and walked over to his house. I must have been there for over two hours. I was just about to give in and then a murmur rose, he was coming down the street. He stopped and was

very genial and friendly to all the fans. He was obviously used to strangers waiting for him outside his house.

We had a chat – he just started talking about the CD in a bendy slip case under his arm. It was an advance copy. He told me that it was the new Verve record and that it was a masterpiece and would be absolutely huge. It was obvious that whatever he'd heard on the album had blown him away. He signed my City shirt on the back and I thanked him and bounced off down the road, back home. By then, he'd met a lot of Oasis fans who'd bought and worn City shirts to impress him but he knew I was the real thing, from my knowledge and probably my accent.
**LIZ TRAY**

22 MAY 1998. I WAS 17 YEARS OLD. MY dad returns from the pub at around midnight and casually says, "I've been offered two tickets for The Verve at Haigh Hall on Sunday, do you want them?" I'd been a fan of The Verve since *A Northern Soul* in 1995. I had never seen them live →

and had been unable to get tickets for Haigh Hall. Did I want them? Did I want them?? Then I rang my mate off the house telephone to ask if he wanted to come with me. . . . The only potential issue standing in the way of us getting in to the country grounds of Haigh Hall was the fact that the tickets were fake.

On the day, the rush of the crowd meant the gate staff were ripping the stubs and throwing them into a large plastic bag quicker than you could see, so we managed to get through, no questions, and sprinted to the bottom of the grounds to get as close as we possibly could.

The Verve came on stage and absolutely blew my head off. I was being hit from all angles as people moved forwards, backwards, side to side. You had no choice but to go with the flow. Whether

you were from Wigan or the surrounding towns and cities there was a buzz in the air for weeks after. **KRIS WEST**

HONESTLY, I CAN'T REMEMBER THE tune to 'Bittersweet Symphony'. But the walk . . . I can remember every part of that swagger. As a teenager I taught myself that walk. Back straight, head up, arms pinned to my sides swinging with each step. A chubby 15 year old flouncing down the road, but it has stayed with me as I've grown older. It has changed and matured with me and it meant that I learned young that you can get away with so much more in this life if you walk with your head up and confidence in your step. **MATT WRAGG**

SINGING 'NEVER EVER' AFTER A bottle of Blossom Hill with my girls in

our cargos before sweating our tits off to 'Block Rockin' Beats'. **ANON**

THE SUMMER OF 1996. I WAS LIVING back in Wigan during the long break after my first year at university. Word arrived, there's a tape. Not just an audio tape – there's a video. The video was borrowed overnight from someone involved in its production with the strict instruction: for viewing only, don't make copies. Copies were duly made. The video was devoured on a daily basis, usually multiple times. The songs, the equipment, the shots, the studio, the people and the clothes. The songs were different in direction but towards other influences we shared; Dylan, Motown and The Stones. The video sleeve simply read *Urban Hymns*.

Home again now and 'Bittersweet' hits. Like nothing I've ever heard before.

Off to Wolverhampton Civic Hall; the best gig I ever saw. The perfect mixture of old and new material. And the pent-up feelings from the time away are unleashed in a joyous celebration of being young and talented. Richard, Nick and Si are on fire and the crowd greets the band they thought they might not see together again as conquering heroes.

Then Haigh Hall looms on the horizon. Getting drunk in the woods. Poole's pies are available and "non-musical" old school friends are bumped into – the true crossover appeal hits home. They're not our band any more, they belong to everyone now. John Martyn's voice and delay-soaked guitar swirls round in the wind. Beck blows our minds with his falsetto and new material. And then the local heroes arrive with 'This Is Music' – two fingers to the swathes of new fans with a big heavy guitar song they probably have never heard before. The band take it all in their stride. They've finally reached the stage they were aiming for and the audience Richard wanted. Wigan is back on the musical map.

**SIMON BERRY**

1997. I'D ARRIVED IN LONDON TWO years previously, moving down the day after I graduated with a First Class (HONS) degree in Photographic Studies. It proved useless in preparing me for working in the industry – it would be another year before I received my first paid photography commission. I was on the dole, doing a bit of cash-in-hand assisting and photographing at jollies and jamborees to rebuild my portfolio. Despite signing on, I was optimistic, as young men in their mid-20s often are. I was in love (I still am), had hair tucked behind my ears and a cluster of ambitious friends.

1996 had hinted at a good life in London. The summer just felt endless, funny and sunny.

1997. Change was happening everywhere and everywhere seemed to be London. Tony Blair land-slid his way into 10 Downing Street.

On 31 August, I listened in bed to an understandably somber broadcast from Classic FM on the morning Diana, Princess of Wales, died. On the day of the funeral, I stooped to photograph the price sticker on the sole of a kneeling woman's shoe as Diana's hearse ghosted past, the bonnet carpeted with flung flowers.

Every fortnight I'd cash in my dole cheque, every weekend I'd head to      ➤

127

Camden to drink in The Good Mixer. I'd then move across the road to the Underworld club and swerve around the dance floor to the sounds of The Verve, Pulp, Suede and Elastica. I could tune in to a fifth terrestrial TV channel. My mobile phone was tiny, used sparingly and not for taking photographs. My pockets were full of change for phone boxes that worked and the fax machine would noisily deliver direct to my mouldy rented flat news of potential jobs. My grandparents were still alive, my shirt was tucked in, a belt was still necessary. Shoreditch was the grubby edge of east London rarely to be ventured into, bars were full of cigarette smoke, you could post-date a cheque and dodge a fare on the bus and underground. 1997, I loved it. **PETER DENCH**

A LATE SUMMER AFTERNOON IN England, the glorious early promise of a new Labour government after so long in the Tory wilderness, the high season of the Britpop explosion which had returned guitar music to the UK mainstream for what felt like the first time in an age, a time of genuine hope. A hired Audi is bombing north up the M6 towards Frodsham – radio blaring, drink slopping over laps, the whole car a haze of cigarette smoke.

Our destination is a house party for someone's 21st and everyone will be drinking. No exceptions. A variety of other recreational substances will also be widely used.

The party is a blur. Christ, the whole decade is a blur now. Shadows of dreams come and go. Embers sparkle and die.

Memories are flattened till only snapshots remain: a huge garden, people disappearing behind a shed the size of a pavilion for a nose-up, mountains of food going almost untouched, and lakes of booze being drained and refilled, drained and refilled, drained and refilled.

And all the time, music is pumping from speakers balanced on windowsills: chart pop, techno and R&B, but mostly it's Oasis, Radiohead, Blur, Elastica, Pulp, Manic Street Preachers, Supergrass, Lush and The Verve. 'Bittersweet Symphony' is played several times, even though it has dropped out of the Top 40 and its successor is due for release the following Monday. The standout song of the summer is as popular as ever.

Sometime around 3 a.m., the music is

a low bass throb and people are starting to drift away or drift off, depending whether they're capable of moving or not. Those still capable of speech in the kitchen are conducting an endless back-and-forth of stoned philosophy through a fog of dope smoke when the door flies open to reveal an elderly Scottish aunt, half-wrapped in a dressing gown, face a mess of half-scrubbed makeup and fresh tears.

"She's dead!" the aunt moans, her accent as heavy as a Billy Connolly caricature.

"Who?" someone eventually asks.

"Princess Diana," she replies, and collapses into sobs.

The person sitting nearest the television switches on BBC1. The news gradually filters through: Diana, Princess of Wales, has been in a serious road accident in Paris.

"Wow," someone eventually mumbles.

One auntie is put back to bed with brandy; the other is left to fill the sudden void in chatter with endless shots of ambulances, police cars and a distant underpass, the anchor discussing the scant facts over and over again with a variety of increasingly excitable talking heads. There is no official confirmation of fatalities, but there is no doubt. Diana is dead.

No one present is particularly royalist; few have anything beyond a passing interest in the deceased. But the event is significant enough to numb everyone into submission. Conversation stutters, then fails. More joints are rolled, but the drugs don't seem to work. Leaving half-empty glasses and unfinished reefers still burning, the gathering disperses, stumbling off to

bed down wherever and with whoever they can. The party is over.

The following morning, the Audi returns south. The music on the radio is instrumental ambience, the Sunday outside is pre-autumn grey and moods are low, introspective . . . anxious. The world has changed and no one knows what it means. Only one thing remains certain, as it always does in uncertain times: when we get home, it will be time for a drink. Something bittersweet.
**DAVID LEWIS**

I REMEMBER IT WAS THE YEAR I graduated university. The final semester of school was a blur of drinking and doing drugs and staying up all night listening to the amazing music coming over from the UK. I remember tripping →

on magic mushrooms after my final exam and just loving life. Once I moved back to New York and started working for my uncle who was a film editor I would spend most evenings sitting in my friend's coffee shop on St. Marks waiting for them to close so we could drink a 40 and smoke a blunt. I remember coming back from that same friend's apartment coming down off of acid when I ran into Richard Ashcroft and lost what was left of my mind. I went to both of their shows at Irving Plaza in November and they were amazing. I remember thinking things were actually looking better for our generation and the world. I can easily fall back into nostalgia these days and it's a sweet trap to fall into but I try to avoid overdoing it. **PAUL SAN FILIPPO**

MONDAY 29 SEPTEMBER 1997 IS A DAY I will never forget. It was a cold miserable rainy morning in Coventry but I jumped out of bed at 7 a.m. with a spring in my step and feeling a few inches taller. . . . I arrived at Woolworths and headed straight to the music section. There in all its glory was *Urban Hymns* right next to the pic 'n' mix sweets. I handed over the cash, legged it back home and listened to it all day long.

It was the best £12.99 I've ever spent. It was the best Monday morning ever. I was loving life and feeling alive.
**NEIL HANDY**

I WAS 19 FOR THE VAST MAJORITY of 1997. In the final year of my teens and enjoying my relatively new life at Newcastle University. I'd discovered mod a few years earlier and Britpop had me in its grip since 1995. I spent whatever spare cash I had on records and clothes from vintage shops across the North.

One abiding memory sticks out – voting for the first time. As a man born in Teesside and with a father who taught me at an early age to never trust the Tories, I was going to take my first voting experience seriously and I was definitely going to vote Labour.

On 1 May 1997, after some lectures in town, a university friend and I went to vote. The weather was glorious in Newcastle and there was a definite feeling of change in the air. We were 19, voting for the first time. An "X" in the Labour box it was.

That night a big gang of us huddled round a TV in my Scouse mate's flat – male/female, Northerners/Southerners, left wing/right wing, working class/upper class – to watch events unfold. One-by-one, Tory seats fell and Peter Snow's map increasingly filled up with red.

I can't remember what time it was

when I finally went to bed, but Labour had already secured an historic victory and Blair was this country's new PM.

A new dawn, a new age.

The next day was even more glorious weather-wise than the day before. As I ambled into town for my first lecture, the sun shone, the birds sang and it felt as though anything was possible. We could change the world, just like that. Dead easy. How naïve we all were.
**DAVID STEEL**

THE VERVE WERE SUPPORTING Oasis, and Liam came out on to the top of the speakers on stage. He just sat and listened for maybe two or three songs. He was just enjoying the music. For a lead act to publicly display that kind of appreciation for their support act was something I'd never seen before or after. That's just how good The Verve

were at that time. Amazing memory.
**ROBERT SOUTHERN**

THE GREATEST GIG I EVER SAW WAS The Verve at Reading Festival. They started playing 'The Drugs Don't Work', which was out when my mother-in-law was dying of bowel cancer and the drugs didn't work. I was sobbing and the young lad next to me took my hand and held it for the whole gig. I'll never forget that.
**TINA ELAINE MAWSON**

MY FAVOURITE SONG EVER, AND STILL is to this day, is 'The Drugs Don't Work'. It's got everything. I was in Magaluf on a stag do and one of the bars belted it out at 2 a.m. in the morning. Not a natural choice for partying holidaygoers but the whole place was singing along. I thought to myself if it can get played in Magaluf in front of a bunch of sweaty 18 year olds

at 2 a.m. and get that reception it really is one of the greatest songs ever written.
**BENNY LAWRENCE**

BEST MATES STAYING IN ON FRIDAY nights in poster clad bedrooms drinking cans of Stella listening to *Urban Hymns* from start to finish.
**OLIVER ROBERTS**

CHRISTMAS RETAIL JOB HELL 1997. 'Lucky Man' being on heavy MTV rotation was the only antidote. The first "affordable" really big screen TVs had appeared and Richard's face beamed out 10 times a day filling a wall. From a nobody to a superstar in six months off the back of three songs and two iconic videos.
**SIMON BERRY**

➔

I MET YOU AT THE SOHO GRAND Hotel in Manhattan, where we were staying. Everyone was in the bar waiting to go to the gig that night. At the airport I'd picked up a suitcase belonging to someone called Bob Formanack whose address label said he lived in Texas. I didn't have any stuff with me and no time to worry about it.

The next couple of days are a bit of a blur. There were limousines and late nights and parties and excess. There were supermodels and Beastie Boys and American record company execs.

By the time we got on the tour bus to go to Boston, Pete's hands were covered in calluses, bandages and plasters – I was blown away by the intensity with which he played and it had never occurred to me that a drummer could sustain such injuries. We got to Boston and checked into the hotel. There was a real buzz there – regular folk staying in the hotel were intrigued by the arrival of a group of rock stars. I got into the lift to go up to our room and a group of middle-aged Americans asked me if I was with "The Verps".

Back on the tour bus that evening, where the band gathered before the gig, the atmosphere was charged. This was my last night with the band before heading home. I was a bit overwhelmed by the experience and ready to leave, back to my job at *House and Garden* and a world of tea and roses; the antithesis of what I'd just experienced.

I'd never been to America before and I'd never been on a tour bus with a rock band. I remember friends worrying that I'd come home in a body bag. I didn't but it took me a while to recover. **GERRY BRAKUS**

I CAMPED WITH THEM IN 1993 AT Glastonbury before they were huge. I shared a tent with Pete. We didn't even have a backstage camping pass. We were camping outside the fence. There was a two-man tent just across from us and people kept going into it but never coming out. After a while we worked out that the tent was the entrance to a tunnel that a group of Scousers had dug underneath the fence. It came up on the other side inside another tent. They were charging £10 a go. Later on Pete got mugged on his way back from performing and he was laughing because he didn't have any money on him, just about a sixteenth of weed. **GEZ GETHINGS**

TO ARRANGE A NIGHT YOU HAD TO systematically call all of your friends to arrange a convenient time and place to meet. Nobody had a phone, so you had to be at a specific place at a specific time or you were going to be spending the evening alone. **BEN SMART**

I REMEMBER FLYING TO NEW YORK for fashion week, knackered from whichever club I'd been to the night before, failing to sleep on the plane because I'd been upgraded and had a bigger-than-anticipated screen to watch films on, and nicer-than-anticipated wine to get drunk on, knowing that HOWEVER TIRED AND JETLAGGED I was upon landing, I was going out that night, because someone had put me on the guest list for The Verve gig at Irving Plaza, and this was basically as exciting as life got.

I think they opened with 'A New Decade'. I think Richard Ashcroft lit a joint. I was up in the balcony, second row, so I couldn't smell it. Maybe it was just a roll-up. In front of me were Kate Moss and Naomi Campbell. Did they like The Verve as much as I did, or were they just There the way models are always There at these gigs; these gigs that seem to define a moment? The Krankies could have been watching this gig and it would still have been the coolest gig I've ever been to. Partly because I was young, partly because I was in New York, partly because I was within touching distance of Kate Moss's hair but mainly because I was in love with *Urban Hymns* and Richard Ashcroft. To hear him perform these songs for the first time, live, was intoxicating.

I will never forget it.

Now, 20 years later, three of them are still among my favourite songs in the world. I can't even listen to them too often because I find them so overwhelming. **LAURA CRAIK**

I DON'T TALK ABOUT THAT TIME much now because I feel like it belongs to me, which I'm sure everyone who lived through *Urban Hymns* thinks too. One day when my son is old enough I'll try and explain how it felt to hear 'The Drugs Don't Work' for the first time. How that band will influence me for the rest of my life, and how we sat around a thing called a "radio" and listened to them play Haigh Hall. **STEVEN JONES**

K720PDS

1997, WHAT A YEAR TO BE ALIVE!
Our village seemed like the centre of the universe. Music was the only religion that spoke to us. Nothing else mattered. We were dreamers. We were heartbreakers. We were lovers. We were fighters. We had it all. We broke the laws, then made our own. We went to Hell, but it wasn't hot enough. We talked to God and He lit the way. It was black eyes and broken noses. It was Adidas, Ben Sherman, 501s. It was Magaluf, Tenerife, Ibiza. It was Cigarettes & Alcohol. We got knocked down and we got up again. We lost our innocence – and found it again.

The party never ended. We had our tribe. The bars and clubs became our churches. We broke the bread, we drank the wine. We had our own Communion. It was ecstasy. We were young and reckless. That summer seemed to last forever. That summer we were all Peter Pan. We were all

Lost Boys. We didn't all make it but we'll always have that summer. That summer we sang our own urban hymns. That summer we were all rock stars. This was our Summer of Love. **GREGORY FAGAN**

20 MAY 1997, I WENT INTO WORK EARLY. I was editor of *The Face* magazine and, as we had just closed the June issue (cover story Lara Croft; among the ups in Barometer "The Verve – They're back!"), I was trying to get some paperwork done before the staff arrived. At 9.30 a.m. Laura Craik, one of the section editors, came directly to my office. "I don't know how to tell you this, or if you already know," she said, "but Gavin Hills is dead."

I did not already know. It turned out that Gavin had been washed off a rock while sea-fishing with friends at the foot of a cliff in Cornwall. The strong currents had

dragged him down, and he had drowned. This fact seemed all the harder to accept because in the previous five years he had visited and written about several international war zones ("Wherever you walk in Sarajevo," he had cheerily written in 1993, "there's always the risk that someone is watching you, fixing his sights and about to pull the trigger.")

Gavin Hills was one of the most distinctive journalists of his generation, and possibly the very best when it came to popular culture. He belonged to a – maybe *the* – dominant arc of 80s and 90s pop culture. A football casual in the 80s, he studied fashion design, began writing for a skate magazine called *RaD,* and then he and acid house happened to each other. He documented those changes (his 1991 story *Whatever Happened To The Likely Lads,* about acid house and football culture,

became a cult in its own right, and was attracting letters to the magazine more than a year after it was published) and the political shifts that bled into and out of them. His writing was honest and funny, and he had that knack of saying what you thought before you were aware that you thought it. His reputation spread, and readers' letters to him began to contain marriage proposals as well as the missives about politics, clubs and trainers.

But this is meant to be about the year 1997, and so I will try to say something about that, particularly something else that happened in the warm, optimistic spring of that year. It's just a personal thing, and I know it will sound ridiculous to a lot of people, but sometimes I feel that we began to lose something then, beginning right at the point when Tony Blair declared the new day had dawned. I can't say exactly what it

was, but it had to do with conscience, with a sense of common purpose, and with swapping a proper respect of other people for a smug pride in our own superficial "tolerance". Somehow, Gavin's death came to symbolise that for me. Somehow, sort-of, I feel like if he was here, he would have been able to make sense of it and if he hadn't known what to do, he would at least have made us feel less depressed. Like I said, I know very well that this sounds ridiculous, but there it is.

If that's all too weird, here's a simpler thought: we could really, really do with Gavin's voice now. Instead of looking back in anger and sadness, let's look up and forward. Here is the ending of his 1993 report from Sarajevo:

*'Do not cease from mental fight, nor let the sword sleep in your hand. The people of Sarajevo are fighting and dying for a*

*multi-ethnic culture. They are protecting their way of life and our way of life. As this century closes, ask, deep down, what all the bullets have been for? Think no longer of hypocrisy, of empires and grand ideals, but only of the good things this world can offer us. The fight is one for tolerance, good music, a nice drink, a decent smoke, the freedom to hang around in bars, to complain about the government, the chance to purchase a tracksuit of distinction, to see Manchester United win the European cup, to watch bad MTV, to play Nintendo. It's complicated, it's a bitch, it can screw up badly, but when we hear the ghost of history calling and the strains of Wagner drowning out Sonic Youth, we must stop switching channels and fight the fools who fight for flags. Click."*
**RICHARD BENSON**

135

# INDEX

**12-13** Westin Hotel, Kansas City, 10 July 1994.

**14-15** Lollapalooza, July 1994.

**16-17** Hard Rock Cafe, Las Vegas, 5 July 1994.

**18-19** Lollapalooza, July 1994.

**20-21** Utah, 7 July 1994.

**22-23** Lollapalooza, July 1994.

**24-25** MGM Grand, Las Vegas, 5 July 1994.

**26-27** Lollapalooza, Bonner Springs, Kansas, 11 July 1994.

**30-31** (Left) Metropolis Studios, London, 1997; (right) Olympic Studios, London, 1996.

**32-33** (Left) Metropolis Studios, London, March 1997; (right) Olympic Studios, London, 1996.

**34-35** Metropolis Studios, London, May 1997.

**36-37** (Left) Metropolis Studios, London, May 1997; (right) Nomis Studios, London, October 1997.

**38-39** Metropolis Studios, London, May 1997.

**40-41** Metropolis Studios, London, May 1997.

**42-43** Metropolis Studios, London, July 1997.

**44-45** (Left) Metropolis Studios, London, July 1997; (right) Sony Studios, New York, October 1997.

**46-47** *Urban Hymns* album cover shoot, Richmond Park, July 1997, except (46: bottom right) 'The Drugs Don't Work' shoot, Chiswick, August 1997.

**48-49** *Urban Hymns* album cover shoot, Richmond Park, July 1997.

**50-51** 'Lucky Man' video shoot, Hammersmith, London, October 1997.

**52-53** Britannia Hotel, Manchester, 11 August 1997.

**54-55** UK Tour, August 1997.

**56-57** Leadmill, Sheffield, 9 August 1997.

**58-59** Leadmill, Sheffield, 9 August 1997.

**60-61** Palais, Hammersmith, London, 14 August 1997.

**64-65** Lemonade Factory Studios, Queenstown Road, Battersea, London, August 1997.

**66-67** Lemonade Factory Studios, Queenstown Road, Battersca, London, August 1997.

**68-69** Lemonade Factory Studios, Queenstown Road, Battersea, London, August 1997.

**70-71** Reading Festival, 24 August 1997.

**72-73** Richard Ashcroft and Liam Gallagher, Earl's Court, London, 27 September 1997. The dates on the agreement giving permission to take photographs (25/26/27 October 1997) are wrong.

**74-75** Richard Ashcroft and Liam Gallagher, Earl's Court, London, 27 September 1997.

**76-77** 'Later with Jools Holland', BBC TV, White City, London, October 1997.

**78-79** Nomis Studios, London, October 1997.

**80-81** BBC Studios, Maida Vale, London, October 1997, except (80: bottom) Nomis Studios, London, October 1997.

**82-83** BBC Studios, Maida Vale, London, October 1997.

**84-85** U.S. visa application photos, Wolverhampton, 13 August 1997.

**90-91** Tour bus, Virginia, 2 November 1997.

**92-93** Tour bus, Virginia, 2 November 1997.

**94-95** Irving Plaza, NYC, 5-6 November 1997, except (95: bottom left) Vic Theater, Chicago, 13 November 1997.

**96-97** Chicago, 14 November 1997.

**98-99** (Left) Phoenix Theater, Toronto, 11 November 1997; (right) tour bus, between Atlanta and Washington D.C., 2 November 1997.

**100-101** Truck stop, USA, November 1997.

**102-103** 'Lucky Man' single sleeve shoot, NYC, 5 October, 1997.

**104-105** 'Lucky Man' single sleeve shoot, 4 October 1997.

**106-107** 'Lucky Man' single sleeve shoot, 5-6 October 1997.

**108-109** 'Lucky Man' single sleeve shoot, Northeast corner of Grand Street and Wooster Street, NYC, 6 October 1997.

**110-111** Detroit, 9 November 1997.

**114-115** Haigh Hall, Wigan, 24 May 1998.

**116-117** Haigh Hall, Wigan, 24 May 1998.

**118-119** Haigh Hall, Wigan, 24 May 1998.

**120-121** Haigh Hall, Wigan, 24 May 1998.

# ACKNOWLEDGMENTS

These pictures were taken a long time ago. Indeed, half my lifetime. Before we put this book together I had not looked at them or thought about them for a long time but I am glad that I did. Not only do they say something about the people featured in them, they also reveal something about me to myself, for which I'm grateful.

Richard Ashcroft, Simon Jones, Nick McCabe, Peter Salisbury and Simon Tong for letting me into the bubble until it was time to leave.

Michael Holden for your perfectly weighted foreword, as well as all the insights, all the highlights, and all the late nights over the last 23 years.

All the good people who kindly sent me their memories of 1997 and the world before the internet arrived to analyse and deconstruct every word we say and every thing we do.

Steve Read and James Brown for opening the door to let me in and John Best for inviting Michael and I along for the ride.

Pete Gunn for always putting my name on the door.

My parents, Sue and Allen Floyd, for letting me be me.

Katie Floyd for being the best sister I ever had and for always being on my side.

Steve Davis, Will Oxtoby and all at Paperhat FTP for patiently giving so much of your time and skill to my never ending requests to scan all that film.

Tony Nourmand and Dave Brolan at Reel Art Press for taking this project on, giving it a canvas to live on, allowing me to come in to your office to endlessly move stuff around on the page and change the font every five minutes. Salman Naqvi for his design and art direction. Alison Elangasinghe for proofing and giving all the words meaning.

Mark Wood and Chas Chandler at Universal Music for suggesting that this was possible in the first place.

Karen Hodkinson and James Morris at Stink Productions for taking it on.

Cosimo d'Aprano for processing and contacting all that film all those years ago, and for teaching me that there is no such thing as "normal" when it comes to silver halide and chemicals.

Finally, for my wife Alice and my daughters Scarlet and Belle. Without you there'd be far less light.

Editor: Dave Brolan
Art Direction and Design: Salman Naqvi
Text Editor: Alison Elangasinghe
Production Assistant: Rory Bruton

First published 2017 by Reel Art Press, an imprint of Rare Art Press Ltd, London, UK
www.reelartpress.com

First Edition
10 9 8 7 6 5 4 3 2 1

ISBN: 978-1-909526-53-2

Pre-Press by HR Digital Solutions

This book is printed on paper Condat matt Périgord, ECF, acid free and age resistant. The Lecta
Group uses only celluloses from certified or well managed forests and plantations.

Printed by Graphius, Gent